Contemporary Posters

Printed in the United States of America
Library of Congress Card Number: 75-41544
ISBN 0-87192-079-4

Printing: Davis Press, Inc.
Binding: Halliday Lithographers, Inc.
Type: Univers
Graphic Design: The Author

10 9 8 7 6 5 4 3 2

Puzzles. An exhibition of braintwisters sponsored by Pepsi-Cola Company for the exasperation of the public, Monday through Friday 9 am-6 pm February 8, to March 21, at the Pepsi-Cola Exhibition Gallery, 500 Park Avenue.

CONTEMPORARY POSTERS
Design and Techniques

George F. Horn
Coordinator of art
Baltimore City Public Schools
Maryland

DAVIS PUBLICATIONS, INC.
Worcester, Massachusetts U.S.A.

BRIDGET RILEY March 2-27, 1965 Richard Feigen Gallery New York

Poster by Bridget Riley. Poster Originals, Limited, New York.

contents

Marisol (Marisol Escobar). Paris Review. 1967
Silk screen, 26'' x 32½''.
Collection, the Museum of Modern Art, New York.
Gift of Page, Arbitro and Resen.

Standing like two sentinels these attractive posters catch the eye of the rail traveler.

The location is static but the poster changes to announce a new event.

Role of the poster

The poster is a familiar and powerful visual force in our daily lives. Fly me — Save today — Don't walk — Enjoy — Join — Learn — Fun, fun, fun — Stop! — The urgent messages of industry, business, merchants, government and institutions are communicated to the wary and unwary alike through the graphic imagery of the artist. We are called upon at a pace that is characteristic of this part of the Twentieth Century to buy, try, drink, think, visit, see, drive, cruise, taste, smell and to respond favorably in many other ways to an endless stream of products, services and events that will enable us to live the "good" life better.

Well-designed or tasteless, shouting or low-key, gaudy or subtle, the ubiquitous poster (also → *Everywhere at once* billboards and signs) takes many shapes and forms as it contributes positively or negatively to our visual environment. Some posters are tall and narrow; others, long, horizontal shapes. Many designs are multicolored; some speak quite eloquently and dramatically with just one or two colors. There are two-dimensional and three-dimensional posters; bright lights and

The No. 15 Limited carries a familiar airline poster to the masses.

A well-designed trash receptacle and an equally well-designed poster affixed to one of its six sides.

moving parts; occasionally, sound. They all serve the same purpose — to get the message across quickly and convincingly to the potential market.

Posters are very much in evidence throughout the dazzling realm of the merchant — on store fronts, interior walls and display cases; attached or painted directly on exterior facades of buildings. They are moved about in the mainstream of urban life on the sides of buses and trucks and on the back of the darting taxi. Available wall surfaces in subways, underground cities, railroad stations, bus and airline terminals are distinguished by the diversity of messages projected by posters they display. Even on the seedy approaches to a big city the irrepressible poster, anticipating our interests and needs, boldly announces the latest plays, movies, entertainment and clothes, refreshment and aspirin.

In addition to the existence of the poster as an important element in the commercial world, it serves a major role in schools at all grade levels and in the community surrounding individual schools. For it is through the poster that students, parents and others can become aware of such things as safety, health, human relations; of events including athletics, plays, dances, club meetings; of holidays and seasonal activities; and of curriculum goals.

The poster, generally a combination of appropriate calligraphy and forceful illustration, is a significant public art form with a specific and unique function in the total spectrum of communications.

This combination of signs, each giving publicity to its own product, camouflages the building and dwarfs the silent monument standing erect near street level.

An old building and a simple, direct message.

Elegant in its stark simplicity this marquee exemplifies the best qualities of a poster.

The Royal Box will re-open in the fall ... But Shepheard's swings all summer!

Disco Dancing & live entertainment nightly throughout the summer
at Shepheard's Park Avenue & 56th Street • Reservations 421-0900

An attractive, stylized poster courtesy Americana Hotel, New York.

*Several posters and torn remnants of yesterday border the bold,
lettered statement of direction.*

*Above a row of ancient windows – bold lettering with an
unmistakable message.*

The 49th. St. Station
is being modernized
Please use
47th. St. entrance.

New York City
Transit Authority

John V. Lindsay, Mayor

LEARN to DRIVE

AUTOMOBILE CLUB of AMERICA
683-6600

FREE PICK-UP   NEAREST OFFICE 1576 B'WAY.   20 LOCATIONS   3 HOUR CLASS

Muller-Brockman, Josef. Der Film Kunstgewerbemuseum, Zurich Ausstellung. 1960. Offset
lithograph, 50¼'' x 35½''. Collection, the Museum of Modern Art, New York. Gift of Kunstgewerbemuseum, Zurich.

"tkts", an unusual treatment, combining structure with bold calligraphy, this arrangement personifies the poster.

A changing sign with additional directions above; the power of the graphic image to control traffic movement.

don't you get hooked!

U.S. DEPARTMENT OF HEALTH, EDUCATION, AND WELFARE, Public Health Service

DHEW Publication No. (HSM) 73-6725

Humor, an effective approach. U. S. Department of Health, Education and Welfare.

Purposes of the poster

The fundamental difference between the poster and other kinds of advertising media is that the poster is designed for an audience on the move. Newspaper and magazine advertising, folders, brochures, booklets, annual reports, catalogs and such usually contain more detailed information and are prepared for the reader to hold in his hands to read at a more leisurely pace.

The poster must capture the attention and interest of the passer-by. Then it must get the message across quickly and directly — in a matter of seconds. The poster must be conceived to motivate the reader to take the intended action through a brief message, packed with punch or even veiled in subtlety. If it does not do this, it has failed in its mission. The poster is designed to proclaim unmistakably the message of its originator. Its primary uses are:

1. To announce an event (plays, festivals, athletics)

2. To promote a service (travel, insurance, organizations)

3. To sell a product (cereal, clothes, typewriters)

4. To develop an attitude (conserve, observe, preserve)

BEHOLD THE
TURTLE!
HE MAKES
PROGRESS ONLY
WHEN HE
STICKS HIS
NECK
OUT

James Bryant Conant

Kersten Bros. Company, Scottsdale, Arizona.

16

even the longest filter doesn't help much!

U.S. DEPARTMENT OF HEALTH, EDUCATION, AND WELFARE, Public Health Service

U. S. Department of Health, Education and Welfare.

EVERYBODY IN THE POOL

BETTER AIR COALITION • 110 East 25th Street • Baltimore, Maryland 21218 • Phone 301/366-2070
Sponsored by U.S. Environmental Protection Agency

Better Air Coalition, Baltimore, Maryland.

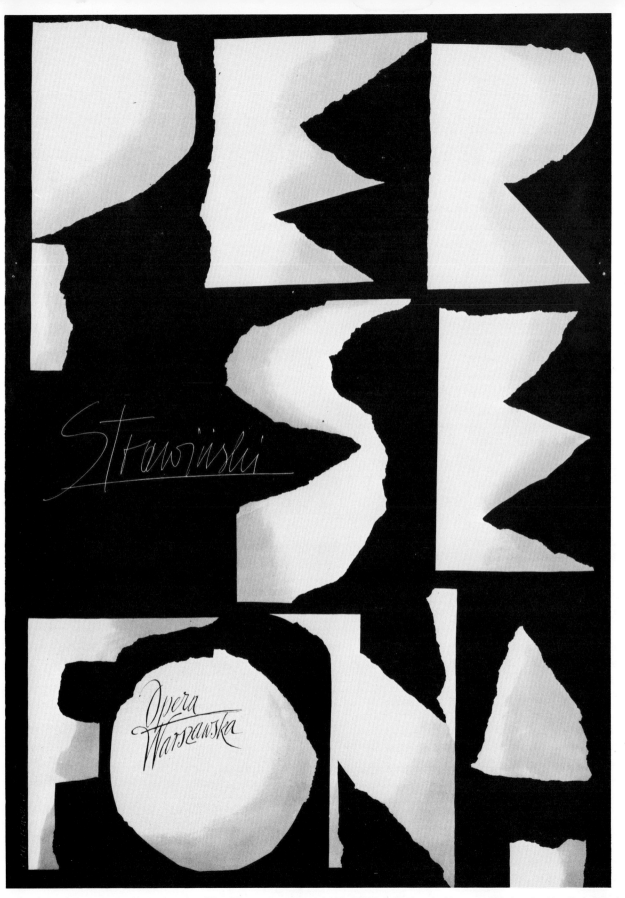

Strawinski Persefona, Rowan Cieslewicz, 1961. Offset lithograph and gravuri, 38'' x 26⅝''. Collection, the Museum of Modern Art, New York. Gift of the designer.

Characteristics of the poster

The fact that the poster is earmarked by its urgent need to sell its message quickly distinguishes it from most other promotional media. As a direct selling agent in the world of commerce, perhaps its only peer is the colorful package, reaching out from the shelves of the retailer to impact the vision of the pushcart buyer in today's supermarket. In many respects the label and the carton have adopted the qualities of the poster. They can serve well as points of comparison in studying appeal as it relates to graphic imagery in poster design.

Supporting the quality of immediacy in establishing communications with the observer, the poster has several characteristics that may be termed unique. These should be carefully considered in the developing of a design for a poster.

1. To be successful, the poster must deliver its message quickly and in a brief, but direct way. Avoid extraneous matter. Incorporate into the design only those elements that are absolutely necessary to tell the complete story.

2. Obviously, the poster must have the capability for commanding attention. This has reference to visual impact, generated by the treatment of words, illustrations, symbols and color. If it fails to attract the attention of its intended market, the poster will be useless.

3. The poster must be convincing. In order to achieve this quality, the designer must know as much as possible about the subject of his poster.

4. Color should be used as a supporting element in the total design. This does not always mean a full range of colors in a single poster. Many times an idea can be presented more effectively with a limited use of color.

5. To be forceful, the poster should reflect an utter simplicity in its design. This quality assists in seizing the attention of the observer and enables him to grasp the message of the poster quickly. Simplicity increases readability.

Aim for unusual treatment of lettering, illustration, symbols and color as they are combined to promote an idea. Uniqueness is a desirable characteristic in any creative design problem; it is conceivable that in poster design, to achieve the uncommon, uniqueness is even more essential.

Posters from Transportation Displays, Inc., New York

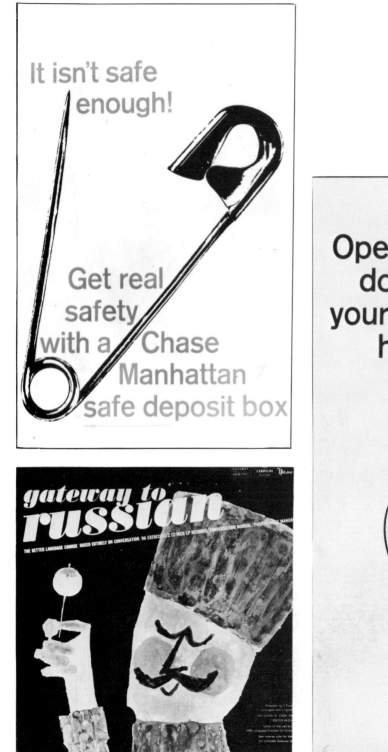

It isn't safe
enough!

Get real
safety
with a Chase
Manhattan
safe deposit box

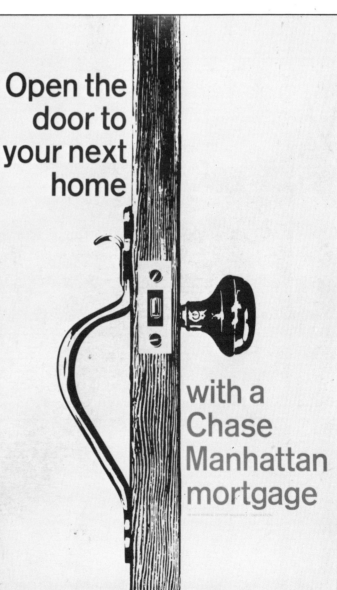

Open the
door to
your next
home

with a
Chase
Manhattan
mortgage

SPEAK SOFTLY

AND
CARRY
A BIG NEWSPAPER
THE NEW YORK TIMES

REMARKABLE
THINGS CAN BE DONE
WITH PAPER

Design qualities and
the poster

Design, or a sense of orderly arrangement is a fundamental factor in all forms of visual expression. A well-organized design elicits from the observer an intelligent and perceptive response to the object being observed; assists in a meaningful, sequential visual movement throughout the design.

Since the poster is comprised typically of two, three or more message components (slogan, illustration, etc.), it is necessary that these parts be brought into a harmonious relationship so that there is no question about the specific idea being promoted. Qualities that are basic to effective, forceful solutions to poster design include balance, unity, movement, emphasis and specific appeal.

27

1. BALANCE — the establishing of visual relationships between the elements (lettering, illustration, etc.) included in the poster in such a way as to project a feeling of stability or equilibrium. There are two different kinds of balance, formal and informal, which produce contrasting visual effects.

Formal balance (also referred to as symmetrical balance) gives the poster the appearance that if it were divided down the middle, one side would be a near mirror-image of the other. A poster design based on formal balance is often thought of as being restful, conservative and somewhat less dramatic than one developed around an informal design. However, some very striking and imaginative posters are excellent examples of formal balance. A generous use of open space, simplicity of illustration, sharp contrasting colors and a careful selection of letter style are contributing factors to the success of a formal-balanced poster.

Save for a sunny stay
Open a Chase Manhattan
savings account

FLY NON-STOP TO ACAPULCO. ◆ EASTERN

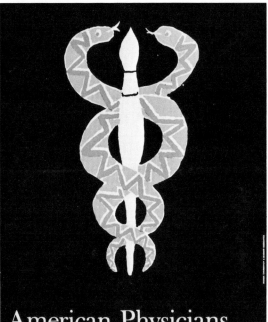

American Physicians
Art Association
an exhibition at
Pepsi-Cola World Headquarters
500 Park Avenue, New York
June 27 to July 7.

Informal (asymmetrical) balance in a poster creates a freer, more active visual effect and undoubtedly is more representative of the spirit of "today". In this approach to design, quite the opposite results are achieved from those of the formal design. A larger element placed near the center of the poster may be brought into balance by a smaller element positioned further from the center on the opposite side. Informal balance provides greater flexibility with increased opportunity for unusual arrangement of the component parts of the poster. Spontaneity, liveliness and animation are typically characteristic of informal balance.

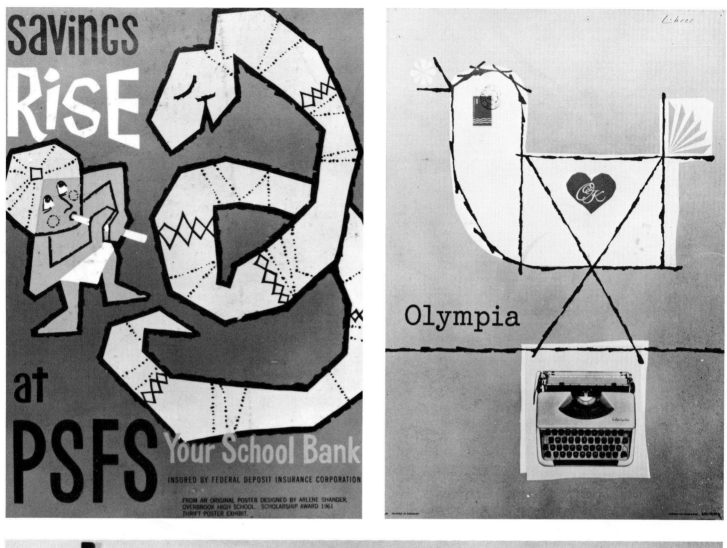

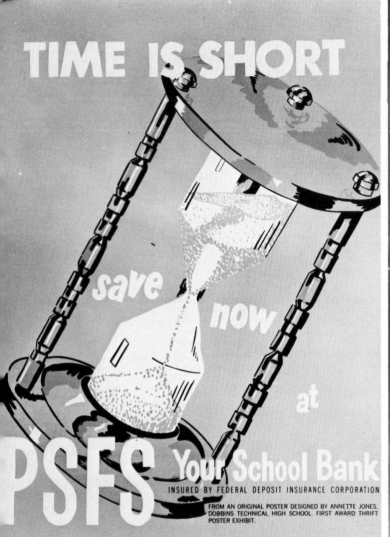

FROM AN ORIGINAL POSTER DESIGNED BY ANNETTE JONES, DOBBINS TECHNICAL HIGH SCHOOL. FIRST AWARD THRIFT POSTER EXHIBIT.

2. UNITY — the arranging of all message units (slogan, illustration, etc.) of the poster to present an appearance of "oneness". Although a poster is designed around two, three or more separate elements, it must achieve a sense of visual unity. Some of the ways in which this may be accomplished include:

a. Overlapping of the message units to establish an easy flow from one to the other.

b. Using background panels, a line or a shape of solid color.

c. Treating the background as a single area of color or open space.

THIS ONE'LL KILL YA.

BETTER AIR COALITION
110 East 25th Street
Baltimore, Maryland 21218
301/366-2070
Sponsored by U.S. Environmental Protection Agency

Better Air Coalition, Baltimore, Maryland.

40th Milan Fair

12-27 April 1962

International
Trade.
Centre

In comfortable surroundings, with the latest
modern services at your disposal, speaking
your own language, you can do business
with fourteen thousand exhibitors from
seventy Countries

Information: Italian Diplomatic and Consular Representatives · Honorary Delegates of the
Milan Fair abroad · Principa! Travel and Tourist Agencies

3. MOVEMENT — The organizing of the component parts of the poster so that the eye of the observer will be led from one part of the poster to another in a predetermined and easy-flowing pace. The poster should be designed so that the various parts of the message are read in the desired order of importance. Movement, slow, fast or moderate, may be visualized in a number of ways.

a. Utilizing of directional lines, an arrow, a row of dots leading from one point to another.

b. Including an action illustration that will point the eye of the observer in the desired direction.

c. Grouping elements so that they appear to move from one part of the poster to another in a natural way.

WASHINGTON D.C.

BRANIFF *International* AIRWAYS

DON'T SMOKE ...

MEDICAL RESEARCH

THE LUNG YOU SAVE MAY BE YOUR OWN

35

Jazz Band Ball, Gunther Kieser, 1963. Offset lithograph, 33½'' x 23¼''. Collection, the Museum of Modern Art, New York. Gift of the designer.

4. EMPHASIS — the assigning of varying degrees of importance to the different elements contained in the poster. If the slogan, illustration and other parts of the poster were all treated with the same importance, the poster would appear somewhat flat. Emphasis may be attained by making one component (slogan or illustration, for example) large and then subordinating all other components to this in the order of importance. The quality of emphasis may be achieved additionally by:

a. Using contrasting background shapes behind the illustration or lettering.

b. Allowing a generous amount of open space.

c. Using contrasting styles, sizes and colors of lettering.

d. Incorporating a large illustration into the design.

Campari, Bruno Munari, 1965. Offset lithography, 77¼″ x 109¼″. Collection, the Museum of Modern Art, New York. Gift of the designer.

5. SPECIFIC APPEAL — The creating of a "feeling" for the theme or idea being presented through the poster. The selection of lettering, color and style of illustration should reflect the specific appeal of the message being presented through the poster.

a. A poster advertising perfume or a hair product for women should be light, delicate, feminine.

b. A poster selling trucks or heavy industrial equipment should be strong, heavy and bold in color.

c. A poster inviting the observer to a winter vacation in the sunny south should be brilliant in color, gay and carefree.

Apply these design qualities to your poster design. Aim for simplicity, legibility and the unusual to attract and to hold attention.

TOYS FROM ALL OVER

An Exhibition at Pepsi-Cola World Headquarters, 500 Park Ave. from January 30th through March 14th. Free European puppet shows daily.

Joan Miro Galerie Maeght, Joan Miro, 1948. Lithograph, 23⅝″ x 17⅛″. Collection, the Museum of Modern Art, New York. Anonymous gift.

Color and the poster

One of the interesting things about poster design is that a generous use of color is not singularly important. Rather, it is the way that color is related to the idea that is significant. The poster designer utilizes color, often on a very limited and reserved scale, only as it contributes to the total force of his design. Very powerful and dramatic results may be achieved through the use of a single color or even through the stark absence of color — black on white, white on black. Therefore, it is essential to understand

Frankenthaler. Poster Originals, Limited.

History & Baltimore

THE U.S.F. CONSTELLATION · FEDERAL HILL · THE FLAG HOUSE
FORT McHENRY · THE CARROLL MANSION · THE MT. CLARE MANSION

Posters above and opposite page, Baltimore Promotion Council, Inc.

color, its characteristics and how it may be adapted to a specific poster idea, on a grand scale or in a restrained manner or somewhere in between these two extremes.

In addition to hue (pure color), color has two basic properties that extend its range — *value* and *intensity* (chroma). Any single color may be altered by mixing or diluting to achieve ranges in *value* from very dark (shades) to very light (tints). Poster colors (tempera) are lightened in *value* by adding white; darkened, by adding black.

Colors in their pure state are at the highest level of their intensity. This dimension of any color may be modified to reduce the intensity by adding varying quantities of its complement. For example, a brilliant red may be lowered in its intensity by adding green. The more green that is mixed with red, the greater its loss of brilliance, even to the point where it may be completely neutralized (gray).

Experiment by mixing white or black paint into a pure color to discover the variety of tints and shades that will result. Then try mixing of complements (red and green, yellow and purple, orange and blue, etc.) to see what happens to a color as you move it away from its pure state. What application does this have to poster design, illustration, lettering?

Another characteristic of color is its psychological impact on the observer. Some colors, such as blues and greens elicit a cool, refreshing, relaxing feeling; while others, including yellows, reds and oranges prompt a sense of warmth and stimulation. Cool colors have a tendency to recede, move back visually; warm colors seem to reach out. Thus, colors selected for a poster will in themselves evoke varying degrees and kinds of response from people seeing the design.

Still another facet of color is its symbolism. Many colors through association with events, experiences, specific uses and ideas of the past and present have acquired symbolic connotations. Some examples of these are: purple and royalty, blue and truth, white and purity, reds and oranges and fire, yellow and the sun or cowardice. Green, yellow and red of the familiar

Museums & Baltimore

ROLAND PARK

1164

B&O TRANSPORTATION MUSEUM · PEALE MUSEUM · MARYLAND HISTORICAL SOCIETY
THE STREETCAR MUSEUM · BALTIMORE MUSEUM / DOWNTOWN · WALTERS ART GALLERY

Music & Baltimore

THE BALTIMORE SYMPHONY ORCHESTRA · ON STAGE DOWNTOWN · PARK CONCERTS · JAZZ IN THE PLAZA

traffic signal universally represent "go", "caution" and "stop".

Color may also be selected for a poster because of its representational quality. This is important when a sense of naturalism is to be reflected in the poster illustration.

Color dynamics, or the effect of one color on another, should be considered when determining the color scheme of the poster. A single color will have varying visual impact, depending upon the way adjacent or surrounding space is treated. Yellow on white, for example, will appear quite different from yellow on black, blue or orange. Closely related colors, such as red and magenta or green and blue-green will produce a subtle relationship. Whereas, colors with strong differences in hue, value or intensity will establish sharp contrasts.

Explore the potential of color, trying various combinations — light with dark, bright with dull, large areas of one color with smaller amounts of another. Relate colors specifically to the poster idea being presented. Do bold, slashing colors generate the desired effect? Or would soft, subtle, low-key colors be more representative of the spirit of the poster idea? One of the best ways to develop a "feeling" for color as it affects the character of a design is to study color as it is used in the vast assortment of advertising media today. Notice the way color is distributed throughout such designs; how color relationships are established for maximum visual impact; varying degrees of contrast in different color combinations; the way color is used to reflect the theme of the design. Then apply these observations to your own poster design.

Child Study Association.

Designed by Heinz Heimann, United Nations Human Environment.

Stamos. Poster Originals, Limited.

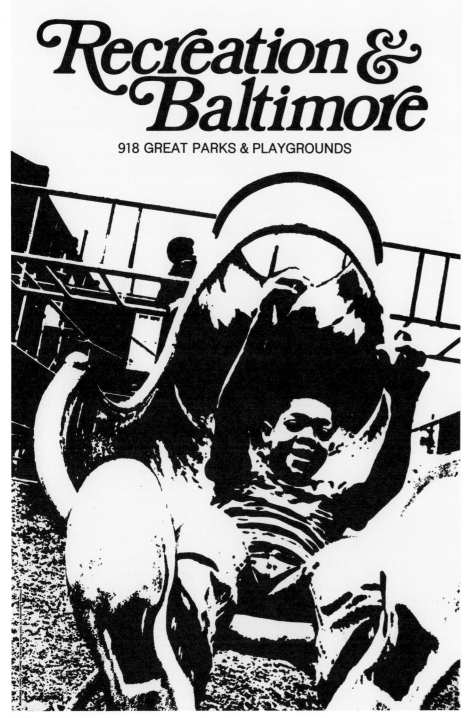

Recreation & Baltimore

918 GREAT PARKS & PLAYGROUNDS

Baltimore Promotion Council, Inc.

Nature & Baltimore

THE BALTIMORE ZOO * CYLBURN PARK * ARBORETUM * EVERGREEN HOUSE

Baltimore Promotion Council, Inc.

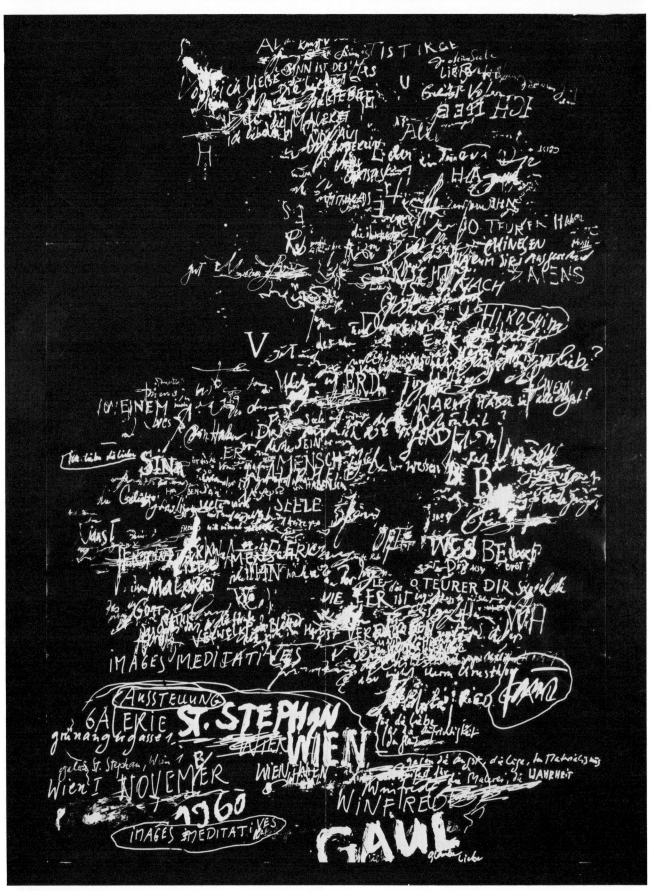

Austellung Galerie St. Stephen Wien Images Meditatives, Winifred Gaul, 1960. Silk screen, 27⅝'' x 19⅞''. Collection, the Museum of Modern Art, New York. Gift of the designer.

AN EXHIBITION IN HONOR OF DR. MARTIN LUTHER KING JR.

Contemporary American painting and sculpture donated by artists to be sold for the benefit of Southern Christian Leadership Foundation

On view October 31 through November 3 at The Museum of Modern Art 11am to 10pm, Sunday 12 noon to 6pm Admission free, entrance at 4 West 54 Street

Richard Anuszkiewicz, Romare Bearden, Peter Bradley, Alexander Calder, Sam Gilliam, Bob Gordon, Adolph Gottlieb, Al Held, Charles Hinman, Richard Hunt, Jasper Johns, Daniel Johnson, Don Judd, Ellsworth Kelly, Lee Krasner, Jacob Lawrence, Al Leslie, Jack Levine, Norman Lewis, Alexander Liberman, Roy Lichtenstein, Richard Lippold, Jacques Lipchitz, Tom Lloyd, William Majors, Marisol, Robert Morris, Robert Motherwell, Louise Nevelson, Barnett Newman, Isamu Noguchi, Kenneth Noland, Claes Oldenburg, Jules Olitski, Ray Parker, Jackson Pollock, Fairfield Porter, Robert Rauschenberg, Ad Reinhardt, Mark Rothko, Bettye Saar, Raymond Saunders, George Segal, Tom Sills, Tony Smith, Theodoros Stamos, Saul Steinberg, Frank Stella, Mark di Suvero, Bob Thompson, Andy Warhol, Tom Wesselmann, H. C. Westermann, Charles White, Jack White, Jacky Whitten, list incomplete

Poster by Peter Gee, courtesy Henri Ghent, Assistant Director Brooklyn Institute of Arts and Sciences, New York.

51

Lettering

Most posters include lettering as an integral element of the total design. Indeed, some posters rely entirely upon the lettered word arranged with combinations of color to present a dynamic, visual statement. More often, however, lettering in the form of a slogan, date, place, name of a product, organization or event is coordinated with an attractive illustration to complete the intended message of the poster.

The lettered word or words to be used on a poster should receive as much design attention as any other element of the poster. Slogans, product names, dates, etc., should be woven into the final design so that they appear to be a natural part of the poster — not as if they have been added to an interesting illustration as an after-thought.

There are many fine examples of lettering and the printed word in the world of advertising that surrounds us (newspaper and magazine ads, folders, record albums, packages, store displays). A closer look at these will help develop an awareness of the effective use of lettering — style, size, color and appropriateness of lettering as it "speaks" for a specific purpose.

Although the names of different letter styles available to the graphic designer present what may appear to be an endless list of variety, most alphabets may be classified into a half-dozen categories — Gothic, Roman, Script, Text, Cursive and Display. A single alphabet in itself has considerable flexibility in that it may be used in standard, condensed or extended form; bold, medium, light; capitals and lower case; capitals and small capitals; all lower case and various additional combinations of these. Generally, however, after a decision has been made relative to the style and direction of the lettering for a word or group of words (slogan), this should be followed through with consistency. For example, if the first letter of a word is condensed, all letters in that word should be formed in the same manner. Intermingling of letter styles and structures tends to reduce the readability of the word(s) and diminish the effectiveness of the poster.

Lettering skills may be acquired only through study of different letter styles and formations; and through regular practice in the construction of letters, words and groups of words.

BOLD LIGHT

STRAIGHT
ITALIC

CONDENSED
NORMAL
EXTENDED

GET TO WORK ON THIS.

Better Air Coalition, Baltimore, Maryland.

The fundamentals of good lettering are described as follows:

1. GUIDELINES
Guidelines are used so the letters in a word or series of words will be uniform in size as well as be kept on a predetermined line. The size of the letter desired will determine the space between guidelines. For capital letters two guidelines are necessary, one for the top of the letter and the other for the bottom. There may be a need for four guidelines when lettering lower-case letters — two for the center body, one for the ascenders and one for the descenders. It is also helpful to use vertical guidelines to keep the letters uniformly straight. Slanted guidelines will assure a consistent angle in italic letters.

2. SPACING
The amount of space between letters in a word should be equal. Due to the irregular shape of some letters, they cannot be spaced mechanically. Good lettering is achieved through optical spacing. In lettering a word, the artist moves some letters closer and some farther apart to get an equal amount of space between each letter in the word. Usually more space is automatically left between straight-edge letters.

3. UNIFORMITY
There should be a uniformity of weight of the letters within a word. In using Gothic letters, for example, all of the letters in a word should be the same thickness. With Roman letters, all the thin strokes should be the same weight as well as all of the thick strokes.

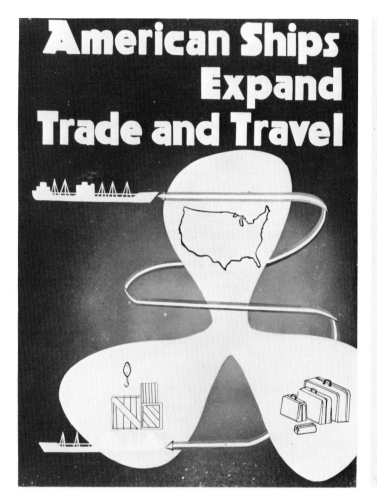

There is a wide assortment of lettering techniques, tools and materials appropriate for poster design. Selection of any single technique may be based upon the specific effect that is desired, as well as the skills and abilities of the designer.

Lettering brushes (single-stroke, flat brushes), metal lettering pens and felt pens are available in many sizes that produce a variety of thicknesses of strokes. Felt pens, containing their own ink supply, may be obtained in almost any color, and shades of single colors.

To become proficient in the use of brushes and pens for lettering, practice vertical, horizontal and curved strokes. An inexpensive paper for such skill-development activity is the classified ad section of the local newspaper. Turn the paper sidewise and, using the lines dividing columns as guidelines, proceed with the exercise. After gaining sufficient confidence and control, apply your skill to the making of letters.

A widely used lettering technique is to block in or draw in the letters first and then paint them. After determining the words to be lettered, style to be used, space in which words are to appear, size of lettering, proceed to sketch in words to fit space. Working over this, draw in or block in each letter accurately and then fill them in with paint. For sharper letters, a ruling pen may be used on the edges before painting them in.

Another technique (using the practice described above) is to letter directly with a lettering brush or pen. This is often referred to as single-stroke lettering. First, draw the guidelines and space the letters in the desired position, then form the letters. The thickness of the letters will be determined by the size of the lettering brush or pen.

What do all 50 top food chains have in common? *FAMILY CIRCLE*

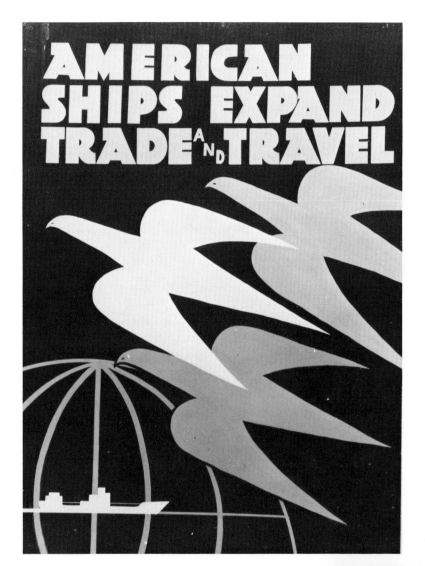

A student using a single stroke lettering brush for poster.

Completing the poster design with brush and tempera (showcard) paints.

60

Letters cut from colored paper can be very effective for use on a poster. Cut-paper letters also give you a certain amount of flexibility that you cannot otherwise get. Once the letters are cut out they may be tried in a number of different ways on the poster before they are pasted down. To assure uniformity of size of letters, first cut a strip of paper to the size the letters should be. Fold this paper in equal parts, according to the desired width of the letters. Then, cut one letter from each fold. The "M" and "W" being wide letters would require the space of approximately 1½ folds. The "I", of course, would be less than one fold.

In addition to colored paper, some rather unique effects may be achieved by cutting letters from printed papers (old magazines, newspapers, wallpaper sample books, gift wrapping paper, to name a few).

An entirely different technique of lettering that may be used in poster design is commercially-prepared, transfer-type that may be purchased (art supply stores) in a vast array of styles and sizes. Complete alphabets are manufactured on plastic sheets. Individual letters may be transferred quickly and easily (to form words) by placing the sheet over the poster board and burnishing the plastic surface.

* s R Q in E EEEE a

Position letter.

Rub over letter with the Chartpak burnisher — be sure to cover all areas and fine lines.

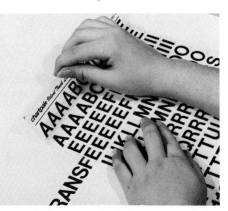

Remove sheet by carefully lifting from corner. For maximum adhesion, place backing sheet over letter and rub again with the Chartpak burnisher.

Spectralegends are the modern way to crisp, clean graphics wherever identification or information signage requires high readability lettering. Spectralegends are pressure sensitive, prespaced and prealigned legends supplied as a single unit. Architectural Graphics Incorporated, Norfolk, Virginia.

Although simplicity in lettering to achieve a high degree of legibility has been emphasized here, there are poster themes that lend themselves to an illustrated type of lettering. Designing with letters, symbolizing and resorting to an expressive style of lettering should be limited, however, to a slogan containing few words. This approach to lettering relies entirely upon the special visual effect achieved rather than traditional readability.

BEVACQUA

The Museum of Modern Art, New York.

WOOD COLD GLASS Yarn HAPPY

One other factor in planning a poster with a slogan of several words is that there may be a need to emphasize one word in the slogan. There are several ways that this may be accomplished:

1. *By making the one word larger than the others.*

2. *By changing the value or color of the word.*

3. *By changing the style of lettering for this word.*

4. *By using capitals for the one word and lower case for the others.*

5. *By underlining the one word.*

6. *By lettering the one word in italics.*

WALK--DON'T RUN!

WALK-DON'T RUN!

WALK--*don't Run!*

WALK-DON'T RUN

DRINK MILK

for HEALTH

CGJSWXYZ

abegjkmt 24

3568 MILK

SUPPORT YOUR TEAM

CBJKVWXabce

fghjkmvz 1234

practice

OFTEN

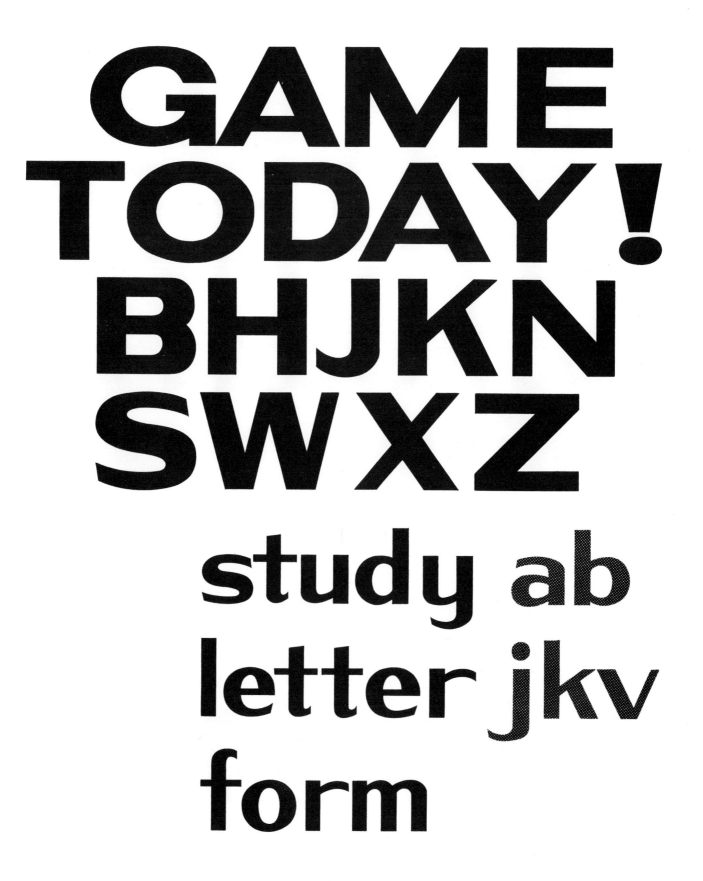

GAME TODAY! BHJKN SWXZ

study ab letter jkv form

Save Money Toda

ABEGHKDJQ

bfghiklrsz 456

PRACTICE

makes makes

PERFECT

Results

Join a CLUB!
DEKMRSTX
WZ bcefkrtv
TRY
OTHER
STYLES

drafting machine...

CHRISTMAS

One Dozen

Find out about the

MEDFORD'S

CHOCOLATE BARK

Swan

A combination of collage, single-stroke felt-pen lettering and a sense of humor gives these posters tremendous impact. George Barrick, Art Department Head, Lake Clifton High School, Baltimore, Maryland.

Collage poster by Kim Mankunas, Thorne Junior High School, Port Monmouth, New Jersey.

A variety of advertising media, including an announcement, package and book cover, showing a marked relationship to the characteristics of poster design; also, extreme simplicity and powerful visual impact.

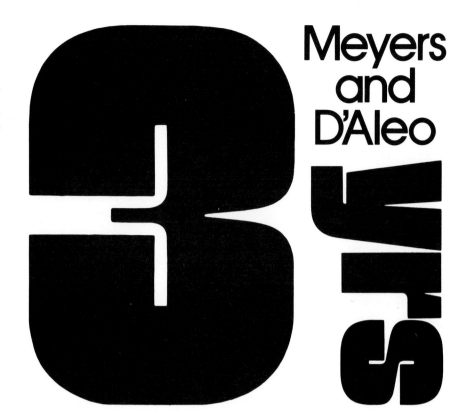

Meyers and D'Aleo

Announcement, Meyers and D'Alleo, Architects, Baltimore, Maryland.

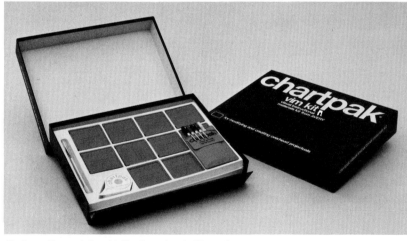

Package, Chartpak Graphic Products, Leeds, Massachusetts.

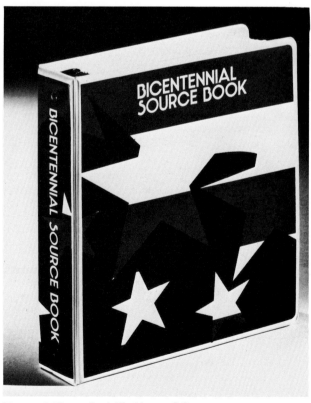

Bicentennial Source Book, Washington, D.C.

Career Education Series, Acoustifone Corporation, Chatsworth, California.

Acoustifone Educational Products Catalog, Chatsworth, California.

Embroidery Kit by Freelance, Lansdale, Pennsylvania.

Poster, Inter Royal Corporation, New York, N. Y.

Products of the advertising world, the striking graphic images on these two pages reflect the qualities of good poster design.

Henry Powell Hopkins
and Associates, P.A.,
Architects, Baltimore,
Maryland.

Dynamic Learning Corp.,
Boston, Massachusetts.

Audio Magnetics Corpora-
tion, Gardena, California.

Biddle Advertising, Chicago,
Illinois.

Illinois Bronze Pow-
der and Paint Co.,
Lake Zurich, Illinois.

Advance Schools, Inc., Chicago, Illinois.

Property of Visual Graphics Corporation,
Tamarac, Florida.

81

Spectralegends, Architectural Graphics, Incorporated, Norfolk, Virginia; a combination of symbols and lettering, resulting in dramatic, unmistakable visual communications.

Poster by Robert Gage, 1952. Collection, the Museum of Modern Art, New York. Gift of Doyle Dane Bernbach, Inc.

Designing the poster

Preliminary to the developing of a design, become familiar with the topic, theme and all particulars that are to be communicated through the poster. The ultimate success of the poster begins with this basic information:

Think in terms of:

1. A meaningful slogan for the topic.

2. An appropriate illustration.

3. Specifics, such as, trademark; name of a product, service or event; a time, place, date; a price.

Generally, a poster will not include all of this information — just that which is necessary to make the message complete. A brief slogan, a dynamic illustration and a minimum of additional reading matter should be the aim.

Other technicalities that should be considered in the pre-design stage are:

1. The size and shape of the poster.

2. The number of colors to be used.

3. The emphasis of the poster.

4. Will it be a "one-shot" design or will it be necessary to make several copies? If the design is to be reproduced, what process will be used (silkscreen, block print, stencil print, other)?

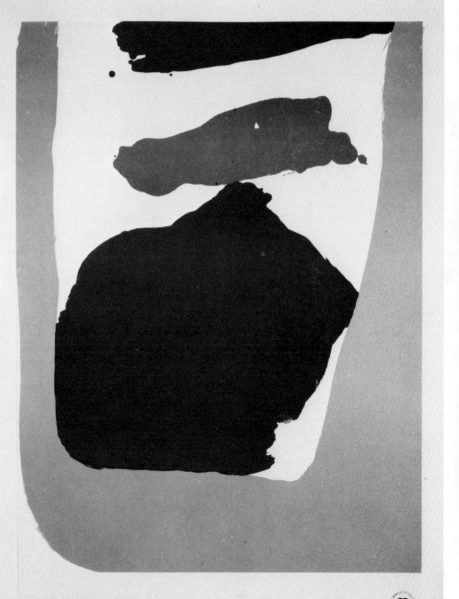

FRANKENTHALER PREVIEW MARCH 16 5-7 PM / TO APRIL 3 1965

Poster by Helen Frankenthaler. Poster Originals Limited, New York.

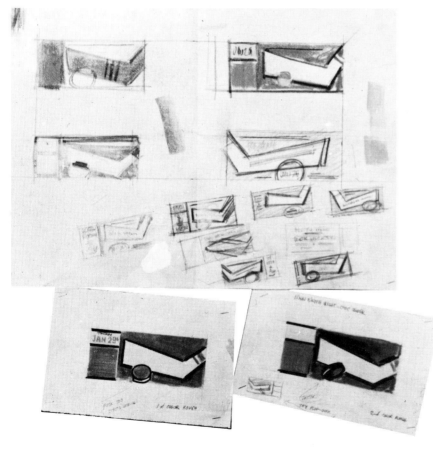

After determining what is to be included on the poster, the basic steps toward completion are as follows:

1. Rough out several small sketches, trying various arrangements of the component parts of the poster (slogan, illustration, etc.). These preliminary sketches, sometimes referred to as "thumbnail" sketches, should be in proportion to the final, full-size poster. One of them will eventually serve as a blueprint for the poster.

a. Explore many design possibilities. Don't be satisfied with the first couple of sketches.

b. Try different effects that may be achieved through lettering and shape relationships.

c. Use different color combinations.

d. Experiment with background shapes, panels, lines of movement.

e. Seek varying emphases from sketch to sketch.

The preliminary sketch is perhaps the most important step in making a successful poster design. It is at this point where critical thinking is brought into visual focus; where unusual ideas are born; where design qualities and color potentials are applied to a specific poster problem. In the preliminary sketch the style of lettering, distribution of color, type of illustration and layout of the poster are determined. The sketches, although developed quickly, should have the appearance of miniature posters.

Above everything else, remember that a poster must attract attention, be easy to read and convincing in its message. To assure this, treat each component part (slogan, illustration, date, etc.) as a unit, arranged into one totally unified design.

A common error is the disjointed arrangement of wording in a slogan. When this occurs, the thought being conveyed can be lost. The slogan should appear in a normal reading position. Excessive angling of words, vertical lettering and splitting of words interfere with readability and should be avoided.

2. For further refinement of the design, invite others to discuss and evaluate the preliminary sketches in terms of visual impact and appropriateness of design to the theme. Select the one that appears to have the best possibilities and enlarge it to full-size on a sheet of tracing paper. This full-size tracing should be complete and correct in every detail.

There are several techniques for accurate pro-portioning of a "thumbnail" sketch to fullsize:

a. If the sketch has been drawn to a pre-determined scale (¼" to an 1" for example) then it will be a simple procedure to multiply every-thing by four.

b. Again, using the same scale (¼" to 1"), block the sketch off in ¼" blocks, the full-size tracing paper in 1" blocks and enlarge the sketch by following the blocks.

c. Another technique is to draw lines on the sketch and the tracing paper, diagonally from corner to corner, vertically up the middle and horizontally across the center. Enlarge the sketch by checking it against these lines.

d. The sketch may also be enlarged by projecting it onto the full-size tracing paper with an opaque projector.

3. Upon completion of the design on tracing paper, transfer it to the poster board and start painting. Refer to the preliminary sketch for colors to be used.

Practice good work habits as you work with paints and other materials to complete the poster.

a. Keep hands clean and free of paint to avoid adding fingerprints to the design.

b. Have plenty of clean water available for mixing colors and rinsing brushes.

c. Keep the ferrules or handles of the brushes clean from paint.

d. The work area should be large; this will allow one to work without feeling cramped and to store the materials being used in the poster.

e. Be sure that the paint is the right consistency, flowing freely from the brush to the poster board. One way for assuring this is to use a scrap of poster board as an intermediate step between the pans containing paint and the surface on which you are painting. Dip the brush into the paint; brush out on scrap board, adding water as necessary; apply to poster.

Poster designed with cut paper.

VARIATIONS IN DESIGN

The procedure for designing a poster at the beginning of this chapter relates more specifically to a two-dimensional poster and the use of poster paints. There are other materials and techniques that may be used to achieve interesting and unusual effects.

a. Working with colored paper, cut a shape to represent the illustration. Then cut strips of paper for the lettering in the slogan. Place these shapes of colored paper on a piece of poster board of the desired size and color. Move them around, trying different arrangements. After determining what is believed to be the best design, complete the illustration and cut letters for the slogan from the strips of colored paper. Other colors of paper may be added to the illustration. Place these parts back on the poster board in the position previously decided upon for final evaluation. Make whatever minor changes that may be necessary and paste the illustration and lettering to the poster board.

b. In addition to colored paper and paint, experiment with materials such as cloth, burlap, straw, raffia, buttons, metallic paper, cardboard, textured papers and boards, found objects and wood scraps and strips.

c. Three-dimensional effects may be achieved by cutting letters out of poster board and setting them out from the background on small blocks of wood. Illustrations may also be cut out and built up on the poster board surface.

The Cutawl, a unique portable power tool, may be used to cut letters and illustrations from heavier material (wall board). These can be assembled to produce three-dimensional qualities.

d. Paper sculpture techniques (scoring, folding, fringing) are possibilities for illustrations on posters. Also, explore the potential of papier-mâché (pulp) for interesting effects.

In Memoriam: Martin Luther King, Jr. by Romare Bearden. List Art Posters, Boston and New York.

The Cutawl is a unique portable power tool with its reciprocating blade capable of turning 360° as it is cutting. With the Cutawl, letters and illustrations for three-dimensional designs may be cut from materials such as heavy cardboard, plywood, plastic. The Cutawl Company, Bethel, Connecticut.

REFERENCE FILE
A very handy source of ideas for poster design may be developed through the organizing of your own reference file to include illustrations, designs and lettering styles that can assist you in designing posters. Layout styles in magazine ads, folders, brochures, booklets and packages often relate very closely to poster treatment and can assist in generating new ideas.

Public Sculptures in Public Places, Bob Cato, 1967, offset lithograph, 15¾″ x 25¼″ x 16¾″, irregular. Collection The Museum of Modern Art, New York. Gift of Bob Cato.

Poster by Ray Lichtenstein. Poster Originals, Limited, New York.

COMMERCIAL MUSEUM

MAY 26 THROUGH SEPT. 4

The Young In Art

3RD ANNUAL EXHIBITION

FEATURING UNESCO AND THE WORLD'S CHILDREN

SCHOOL ART LEAGUE
PHILADELPHIA · PUBLIC · SCHOOLS
FREE - 34th and CONVENTION AVE
BUS ROUTES 39 - 40 - 42

Reproduction techniques

A single poster design may be reproduced many times by one of several available printing processes. When a poster is to be reproduced in vast quantities commercially, it is often done by the letterpress printing process or by planographic printing, also known as offset lithography. Since it is unlikely that either of these two methods would be used for most school purposes it is sufficient to merely mention them here. It is recommended, however, that a visit to a letterpress and an offset printing plant would be desirable to acquire an understanding of the steps involved in each printing process. Such an experience would also point out the requirements for the preparation of art work for a poster to be reproduced by either of these two methods.

While letterpress and offset printing would be limited to the commercial printer, the following comparatively simple methods for duplicating a poster can be developed within the realm of the school:

Silkscreen Printing

Stencil Printing

Block Printing

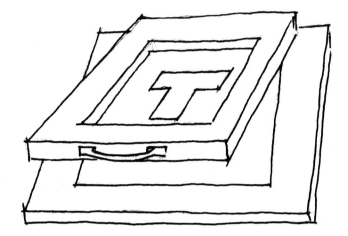

SILKSCREEN PRINTING

Silkscreen printing is a widely used stencil technique for reproducing a design. The design may range from one color to a number of colors. It may be reproduced on paper, poster board, wood, metal, plastic, glass, cloth or on many other kinds of surfaces. The material on which the design is to appear may be in either a two-dimensional or three-dimensional form. Posters, car cards, displays and illustrations used in advertising are often reproduced by the silkscreen printing process. It is also a very popular medium for applying color and design to toys, games and furniture; labels on bottles, cans, plastic containers, boxes.

Basically, the silkscreen printing process is the forcing of paint through a piece of stretched silk on which a design has been applied. The design is formed on the silk by blocking out some of the mesh and leaving the part to be printed open. The illustration shows a screen prepared to print the letter "T". The area around the "T" has been blocked out and the silk forming the "T", left open. The following steps are required to reproduce the "T" the number of times desired:

1. Screen placed over paper on which "T" is to be printed.

2. Silkscreen paint poured at one end.

3. Paint pulled over the screen by means of a squeegee.

4. Screen lifted showing "T" printed on paper.

The same "T" may be reproduced in reverse by blocking out the "T" on the silk and leaving the area around it open. With this approach, the background would be printed and the "T", itself, would assume the color of the paper on which it is being printed. Although there are many kinds of materials and numerous techniques involved in silkscreen printing, including photography, the example shown here is fundamentally the silkscreen printing process.

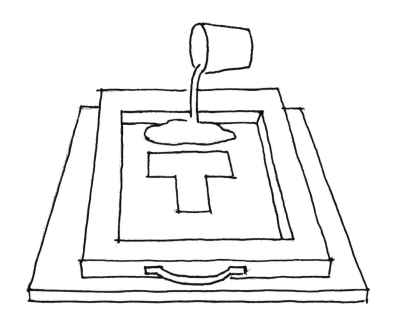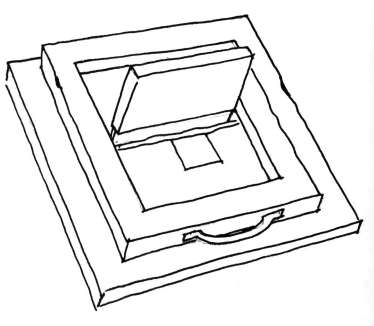

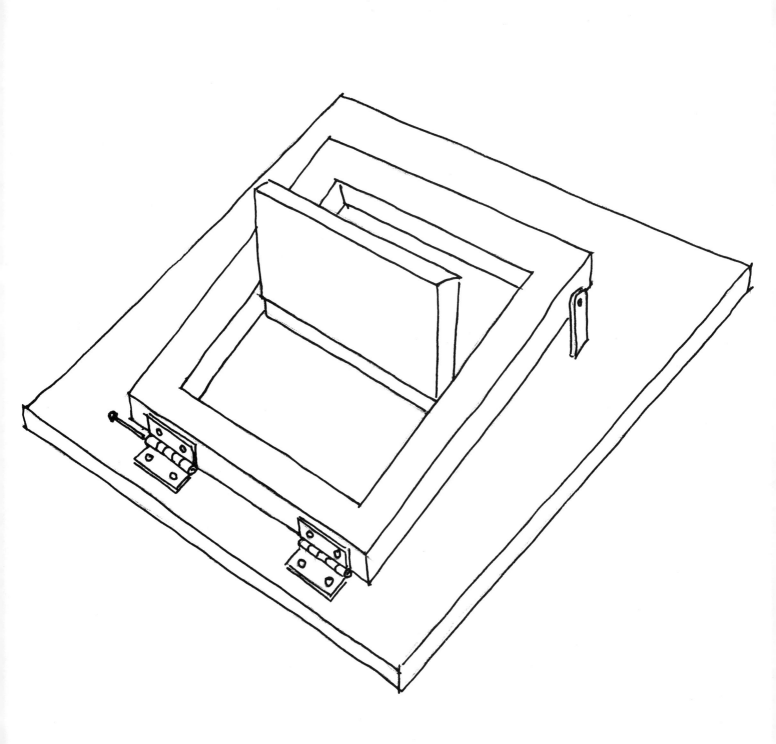

EQUIPMENT, TOOLS AND MATERIALS

The following equipment is necessary for silk-screen printing:

1. BASEBOARD
The baseboard may be either a piece of heavy plywood or an old drawing board. It should be larger on all sides than the printing frame, which is to be mounted on it.

2. PRINTING FRAME
A printing frame is a simple, wooden frame on which the silk is stretched and stapled. It should be larger than the design which is to be printed. To be safe, allow 2 to 3 inches extra space all the way around the frame.

3. LOOSE-PIN HINGES
Loose-pin hinges are used to attach the printing frame to the baseboard. This type of hinge is suggested because it allows easy removal of the printing frame from the baseboard. This is important, particularly when the design is more than one color, therefore requiring two or more printing frames.

4. SQUEEGEE
The squeegee, made of rubber, is used to pull the paint across the screen. Its size is determined by the size of the screen. The squeegee should be large enough so that the paint can be pulled across the surface of the silk in one stroke.

5. SILK
While other fabrics, such as organdy, may be used, silk is recommended. It is durable and allows one to attain a uniform, good quality reproduction. A medium-fine mesh silk will serve the purpose for most school needs. The silk must be stretched drum-tight on the frame. This may be accomplished by pulling it tight as it is being stapled to the side of the frame.

6. Tools that should be available for silkscreen printing would include: scissors, cutting knives, brushes, stapler, steel straight-edge.

7. The following materials are necessary for silkscreen printing:

a. Silkscreen paint, assorted colors. Silkscreen paint may be either oil or water base.

b. Adhering fluid. This is used in transferring a design made with stencil film to the silkscreen.

c. Removing fluid. Removing fluid is used to remove stencil film from the silk.

d. Stencil film. This is a film of colored lacquer laminated to a sheet of glassine paper.

e. Transparent base. Transparent base is added to silkscreen paint to improve the working quality of the paint. It also gives a transparent quality to the paint and is used when there is over-printing in the design.

f. Extender base. Extender base is used to cut the cost of printing. It may be added to paint to extend the colors without reducing their strength.

g. Glue.

h. Tusche.

i. Water tape and masking tape.

j. Stencil filler.

k. Reducers. Kerosene or varnalene may be used to reduce the consistency of oil base silkscreen paint. They may also be used in the cleaning of the screen.

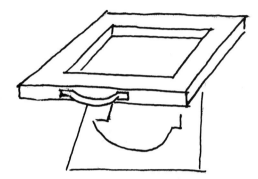

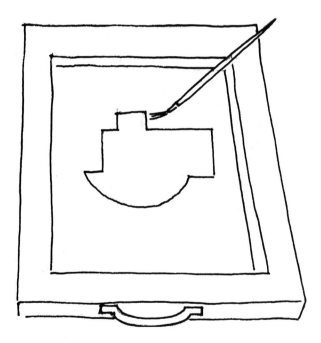

SILKSCREEN STENCILS
There are several techniques for preparing the screen to duplicate a design.

1. THE BLOCK-OUT METHOD
- Place the design to be printed beneath the silkscreen.
- Trace the design to be printed on the silk.
- Block out the silkscreen around the design with stencil filler. When the stencil filler dries, the screen is ready for printing.

2. PAPER STENCILS
This method is used for short runs and may be described as follows:
- Cut design out of paper.
- Place a sheet of waste paper on the baseboard beneath the screen.
- With the screen raised, lay the paper stencil in position.
- Lower the screen and pour silkscreen paint on one end.
- Squeegee the paint over the screen and the paper design beneath it will adhere to it.
- With the paper stencil now adhered to the screen, it is ready for printing.

3. THE TUSCHE METHOD.
With this technique the design is actually painted on the screen with liquid tusche, which provides the designer the opportunity to stipple, spatter or dry-brush to get unusual effects.
- Place design to be printed beneath screen.
- Transfer design to screen, using Tusche.
- After design is complete, coat the entire screen with a mixture of water and glue (approximately ½ and ½).
- When glue is dry, wash the screen on both sides with kerosene. Those areas where Tusche has been applied will wash off, leaving the desired design.
- Place screen on a piece of newspaper and wash further to remove all particles of Tusche. The screen should then be ready for printing.

AFRICA PAN AM

American Airlines.

4. STENCIL FILM

This is a film of colored lacquer laminated to a sheet of glassine paper so that it can be cut and peeled off. The film must be cut without cutting the glassine backing. When using the stencil film technique, the part that is peeled away is the part that will be printed.

- Tape a piece of stencil film over the design.
- With a stencil knife, cut around the design and peel off areas to be printed. (If the design is printed in one color, cut the entire design on one piece of stencil film. If it is more than one color, a separate piece of film will have to be used for each color.)
- Place completed film stencil under the silk-screen frame.
- With a small rag, apply adhering fluid to a portion of the screen. Rub over this briskly with a dry rag. Continue until entire screen is covered and film is adhered. Do not oversoak the screen with adhering fluid or the film will dissolve.
- Stand screen on edge to dry. After it has dried, peel off the glassine backing sheet.
- Fill in the open part of the screen with paper tape. Use stencil filler to touch up spots on the design. The screen is now ready for printing.

BLOCK PRINTING

Wood, rubber and linoleum blocks are often used commercially to reproduce posters and car cards. These materials may be used in duplicating school posters. For short runs a design may be cut from heavy cardboard and mounted on wood. In each case, a separate block must be prepared for each color in the design.

GET TO WORK ON THIS.

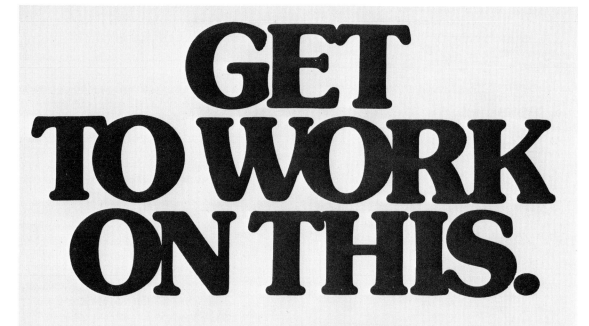

Better Air Coalition, Baltimore, Maryland.

103

104   *Better Air Coalition, Baltimore, Maryland.*

GUIDE TECHNIQUES

Once the prepared screen is hinged in place on the baseboard it will always come down on the same spot. However, it is important that the paper or poster board, on which the design is being printed, is positioned properly beneath the screen each time. This is even more critical when silkscreening a design having two or more colors. There are two methods suggested here for assuring accurate registration:

- When printing on poster board, squares of the same thickness as the poster board may be used as guides.
- Tagboard or heavy paper, cut and folded, also serves well as registry guides.

CARE OF THE SILKSCREEN

If there is to be a rerun of a design, the screen may be stored with the design on it. Be sure that the printing inks have been thoroughly removed from the screen before storing.

On the other hand, a design may be removed from the silk and the same screen used again with another design. The method for cleaning the silk would depend on the method used in applying the design in the first place. For example, when stencil film is used on the silk a special removing fluid must be used to wash the design off of the silk. Lacquer-base stencil filler may be cleaned from the silk with removing fluid. Warm water and soap will wash water-base glue from the silk.

With proper care and thorough cleaning, the silk may be used over and over many times.

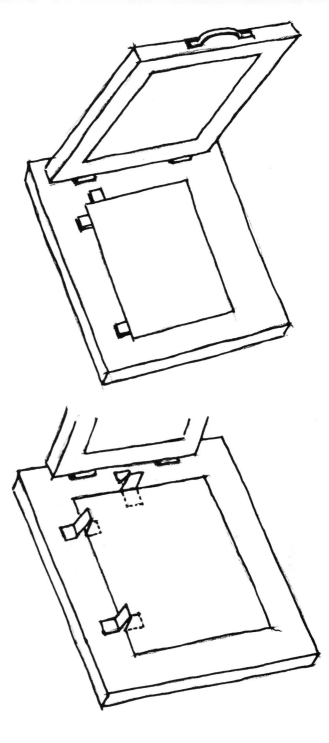

Sequence of steps required in silkscreening a poster in four colors.

STENCIL PRINTING

The stencil technique may be used in the designing of a single poster as well as in making duplicates of a poster. It is basically the blocking out of some areas of a design while applying a specific color to another area. In stencil painting or printing, the paints may be applied by an airbrush, a hand air gun or stencil brush. With this technique it is possible to get graded tonal qualities in the design. Spattering and stippling are also characteristic of stencil printing.

In reproducing a poster design, the stencil printing technique is recommended when there are a small number of duplicates to be made.

1. Prepare the master poster design in color, actual size, following the suggestions discussed in preceding chapters of this book. A poster to be reproduced by this method should be kept relatively simple.

2. Cut a stencil for each color. For example, a background shape or an illustration may represent one color in a two-color poster and would require one stencil. The lettering may represent another color, calling for an additional stencil. The stencil may be made by tracing that part of the design represented by one color onto a piece of heavy paper and cutting it out with a sharp knife. Acetate may also be used for stencils. Lay the paper or acetate over the master poster design and cut away that which would form one color. Repeat this for the second color and again for each additional color.

3. Using rubber cement, fix the first stencil to a piece of poster board.

4. The color for this stencil may then be applied with an airbrush, a hand spray gun or a stencil brush.

5. After the paint is dry, remove this stencil and proceed with the stencil for the second color.

When making several duplicates of a poster by the stencil method, print all of one color first. Then go back and repeat this step for each stencil.

Posters to be reproduced by this method should be designed with areas of flat colors and bold lines in lieu of fine shading and delicate lines.

One marked difference between this printing method and the two others described in this chapter is that the blocks are prepared in reverse. In silkscreen printing and stencil printing the color is applied through the screen or stencil. In block printing the color is applied from the raised surfaces of the block.

1. Prepare the master design for the poster in color, actual size.

2. Make tracings for each color.

3. Reverse these tracings and transfer them to the block (wood, rubber, linoleum, cardboard).

4. Cut the block.

5. Print the poster, one color at a time.

Block printing is done with a variety of types of equipment, from the relatively simple hand press to the somewhat complex letterpress, used by commercial printers. Basically it is a matter of inking the prepared block, placing it in position against the poster board, applying pressure and removing it.

In duplicating a poster by the block printing method, print all of one color at a time.

ADDITIONAL SUGGESTIONS

The methods for reproducing posters described here have considerable versatility and lend themselves to experimentation. While it is important to know each process and the basic steps involved, there are many possibilities. Some suggestions along this line are:

1. In the process of printing a poster, change the color combinations. Even though the same basic design may be used throughout a single "run", changes in color combinations will give added variety.

2. Try using two different colors at the same time on the same silkscreen. Note the unusual and changing, blending effects.

3. Experiment with using contrasting colors at the same time on a single block.

4. Combine the different processes. For example, a background effect may be sprayed through a stencil and the illustration, block-printed on top of this.

5. Combine hand lettering with one of the processes.

6. Use shapes of colored paper in combination with one of the processes.

Poster-related signs and symbols from the past are interesting and direct in their message. Restored Towne of Smithville, New Jersey.

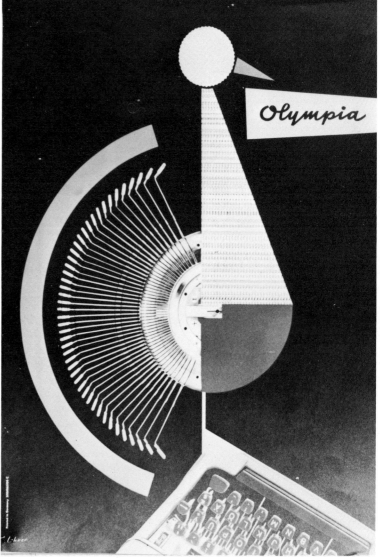

ACKNOWLEDGEMENTS

I am most appreciative to those who supplied me with poster designs. Examples of modern poster design and their use will help to motivate the reader of this book. Individuals and institutions providing materials are:

The Museum of Modern Art, N.Y.; Poster Originals, Limited, N.Y.; List Posters, Boston and New York; Brooklyn Institute of Arts and Sciences, N.Y.; U.S. Department of Health, Education and Welfare, Public Health Service; Better Air Coalition, Baltimore, Md.; Baltimore Promotion Council, Inc.; Transportation Displays, Inc., N.Y.; the New York Times; the Cutawl Co., Bethel, Conn.; Chartpak Graphics Products, Leeds, Mass.; Americana Hotel, N.Y.

Also, George Barrick, Art Department Head, Lake Clifton Senior High School, Baltimore; Laura De Wyngaert, art teacher, Thorne Junior High School, Port Monmouth, N.J.; Bill Meyers, Meyers and D'Aleo, Architects, Baltimore; Fred T. Knowles, President, Architectural Graphics, Inc., Norfolk, Va.; and Kersten Bros. Company, Scottsdale, Ariz.

Poster by Ben Shahn. The Museum of Modern Art, New York. Gift of the CIO Political Action Committee.

Koshimaki Osen, Tadanori Yokoo, 1966, silk screen, 41½" x 29⅜". Collection, The Museum of Modern Art, New York. Gift of the designer.